JOHN LENNON
Fighting for World Peace

2

JOHN LENNON

Fighting for World Peace

Enslow Publishing
101 W. 23rd Street
Suite 240
New York, NY 10011
USA
enslow.com

Jeff Burlingame

Published in 2018 by Enslow Publishing, LLC.
101 W. 23rd Street, Suite 240, New York, NY 10011

Library of Congress Cataloging-in-Publication Data

Names: Burlingame, Jeff, author.
Title: John Lennon : fighting for world peace / by Jeff Burlingame.
Description: New York : Enslow Publishing, 2018. | Series: Rebels with a
  cause | Includes bibliographical references and index. | Audience: Grades 7-12.
Identifiers: LCCN 2017027841 | ISBN 9780766092600 (library bound)
  | ISBN 9780766095649 (paperback)
Subjects: LCSH: Lennon, John, 1940-1980—Juvenile literature. | Rock
  musicians—England—Biography—Juvenile literature. | LCGFT: Biographies.
Classification: LCC ML3930.L34 B85 2017 | DDC 782.42166092 [B] —dc23
LC record available at https://lccn.loc.gov/2017027841

Printed in China

To Our Readers: We have done our best to make sure all website addresses in this book were active and appropriate when we went to press. However, the author and the publisher have no control over and assume no liability for the material available on those websites or on any websites they may link to. Any comments or suggestions can be sent by email to customerservice@enslow.com.

Portions of this book originally appeared in *John Lennon: "Imagine"* by Jeff Burlingame.

CONTENTS

INTRODUCTION

I t had been several hours since the girls had screamed and sobbed for them, and 3,500 miles since their plane had left the London airport, each second of its ascent shrinking the thousands of song-singing Britons below, until their "We Love You, Beatles" signs no longer could be seen from the windows of Pan Am Flight 101.

The pre-takeoff passion on February 7, 1964, had been expected. The Beatles were England's biggest rock-and-roll band, heading off to America for the first time to try to succeed in a country where so many other British bands had failed. America was a difficult market to penetrate because rock-and-roll music had been invented there. It was home to groundbreaking musicians such as Chuck Berry, Bob Dylan, and Elvis Presley. Those were the people the four Beatles had grown up listening to and had drawn inspiration from.

As New York City came into view, the Beatles' outspoken leader, John Lennon, had questions. He wondered exactly what the trip to America would hold

On February 7, 1964, the Beatles arrived in New York City, starting what would become known as "the British Invasion," with British musicians taking over the pop charts in the United States.

Fans went crazy for the Beatles, and "Beatlemania" quickly spread. Here, fans are shown being restrained by police officers while waiting for the Beatles to arrive at New York's Kennedy airport.

for him and his three bandmates. Years later, Lennon said, "We didn't think we stood a chance."[1]

Lennon's fears may have been calmed had he known exactly how much publicity he and his band had been receiving in the United States. They knew that just a few days earlier their single, "I Want to Hold Your Hand," had become the number one record in America. But they did not know their record label had spent $50,000 on a campaign to spread word of their impending arrival. They did not know that five million "The Beatles Are Coming" stickers had been plastered across the United States, nor did they know that 50,000 people had applied for the 728 seats available to see them perform on TV.

Roughly 10,000 people, mostly teenagers, were waiting at the John F. Kennedy International Airport terminal when the band arrived. Screams filled the air as the Beatles exited the plane and were ushered to a press conference inside the airport. The room was full of reporters, who began firing off questions as soon as the band members walked in. It was near chaos, but with his first words, Lennon took control: "Everybody just sharrup [shut up]."[2] The media applauded, then did just as Lennon asked. The questions came at them rapid-fire, and the Beatles handled them all with the sarcastic wit that had helped make the band so endearing in Europe.

The band's most immediate questions had been answered. America had turned out to see the Beatles, and eventually fell for them as hard as their own country had. But Lennon was not satisfied with all that. He also had deeper issues on his mind. Namely, were people really listening to his music, or were they just caught up in the hype of it all?

For Lennon, the answer was clear. He said, "What we generated was fantastic when we played straight rock, and there was nobody to touch us in Britain. But as soon as we made it, the edges were all knocked off.... [W]e made it very, very big. We sold out.... The Beatles' music died then.... We killed ourselves then to make it—and that was the end of it."[3]

But before there could be an end, there had to be a beginning. Lennon's had come nearly a quarter-century earlier in a war-torn English city as gritty and staunch as he.

1

Genius and Pain

At the time of John Lennon's birth on October 9, 1940, his country of England was in the midst of the infamous Battle of Britain, the name given to Germany's all-air campaign against England. The German air force eventually was held at bay by Britain's Royal Air Force, but not before substantial damage was inflicted on England. As a major seaport located on Britain's northwestern coast, John's hometown of Liverpool—and its many manufacturing and shipping areas—was one of the most-attacked and most-affected areas of the entire war.

Many believe John's birth at the Oxford Street Maternity Hospital came during the middle of a ferocious air raid, and that his mother, Julia, was in labor as her relatives rushed through Liverpool's darkened streets—covering their ears from the piercing air-raid sirens—to be there for her.

Even if he was not born during an actual air raid, the effects of war certainly were all around John. Photos from the time show many holes in Liverpool's skyline, where multistory buildings used to stand. Burned-out buildings and blackened rooftops dot the landscape. The Luftwaffe air raids left Liverpool forever scarred.

John Winston Lennon was named in part for the British Prime Minister Winston Churchill. Though Churchill was a popular war hero, Lennon would come to despise his connection to the man when he later grew up to become an anti-war activist.

John's middle name, Winston, was given to him in honor of Britain's recently appointed prime minister, Winston Churchill, the half-American war expert who held England's fate in his hands. It was a name the young child would grow to hate for its connection to a man so linked with war.

John's father, Alfred "Alf" Lennon, was not at the hospital for his son's birth. He was away at sea, where he worked as a ship's steward in the merchant marines. His absence at his first son's birth was not surprising. Alf had been away for much of his two-year marriage to Julia, a fact the new mother's family took much pleasure in noting, because they did not care much for Alf. Alf's absence was a case of history repeating itself. His own father had died when he was young, and his mother—though she worked from dawn to dusk to try to do so—could not support him and his five siblings. Alf Lennon was sent to live in a Liverpool orphanage, leaving there at age fifteen for a job as a waiter on a ship.

No one in the family could understand why Julia would marry someone like Alf, because she had been raised by a family whose means far surpassed those of her future husband. Like Alf Lennon, Julia's father, George Stanley, also made his living off the sea. But George Stanley's work at the Liverpool and Glasgow Tug Salvage Company placed him in the company of people higher up the social ladder.

Though her family did not see any redeeming qualities in Alf Lennon, Julia had almost immediately. His intellect and his wit had struck her, along with his boyish good looks. Julia was able to see past Alf's short stature, caused by a battle with rickets as a child. And Alf also was a talented musician who, at fourteen, had run away from his orphanage to join a children's musical show—and was severely punished upon his return. Alf sang and played the banjo, the latter a skill which Julia herself had learned from her grandfather.

Coming Together, and Apart

Julia and Alf had met in 1930, when Alf was fifteen and Julia fourteen. Their courtship, lengthened by Alf's stints at sea, lasted eight years. During Alf's time ashore in December 1938, he and Julia secretly wed at the Mount Pleasant Registry Office. The honeymoon did not last long before Alf was back at sea.

Julia grew restless alone, and began venturing out at night to Liverpool's numerous pubs and dance halls. There, in 1944, she met a Welsh soldier named Taffy Williams, and became pregnant with his child. John was four years old at the time.

For a while, Alf Lennon remained oblivious to his wife's extramarital relationship. Still away at sea, he continued sending both romantic letters and paychecks home. But he had his own major issues to deal with. Twice he was sent to prison for various misdeeds and, at one point, the British navy mailed a letter to Julia saying they had no idea where her husband was. It was not until late 1944 that he turned up at home, only to discover his wife was pregnant by another man. Alf tried to save his marriage and keep the family intact, even offering to raise the child as his own and forgive his wife for her indiscretions. None of it worked. Julia Lennon no longer had feelings for the man she had been together with for more than a decade. Alf returned to the sea.

When Julia gave birth to a daughter, Victoria Elizabeth, in June 1945, her embarrassed father suggested she give the child up for adoption. Julia reluctantly agreed and soon returned to her partying ways.

The following year, John's mother became involved with a somewhat-older hotel worker named Bobby Dykins, and the couple soon moved in together. Julia's family and friends did not like Dykins, either. They described the new suitor as having a violent temper with "a very short fuse. Julia knew when to get out of his way, but occasionally he would lash out and slap her."[1] John later said one of his most-vivid childhood memories included the time when "my mother came to see us in a black coat with her face bleeding."[2]

Partly because of the abuse he had to witness at home, John was forced to make a tough decision the summer prior to his sixth birthday. His father had quit his job as a ship's steward—where he was regularly traversing the Atlantic between southern England and New York—and had returned to Liverpool to take his son for the day. He took John to the northwestern town of Blackpool, England, and lavished junk food and gifts on the boy. The day-long adventure turned into weeks, and Alf still had not returned John home. Angered and upset, Julia and Bobby Dykins eventually found out where the pair was, and they traveled to Blackpool to take John back. When they got there, Alf asked his son a difficult question: Did he want to go with his mother or stay with his father? John was torn but eventually chose his mother.

Julia took her son back to Liverpool, but not to live with her. Instead, she delivered him to his aunt Mimi's house, where he would remain for the rest of his childhood. John later said, "I soon forgot my father. It was like he was

15

dead."[3] John would not see his father again until after he had become famous. As for his mom, John said he always continued to miss and love her.

John's aunt had her reasons for keeping her youngest sister at a distance. She felt that she—along with her husband, George Smith—offered her nephew the best chance at a proper, trouble-free upbringing.

Aunt Mimi, as John called her, was the opposite of her younger sister, Julia. She was childless and stubborn, but responsible, and determined to offer her nephew a stable, if strict, upbringing. John initially thrived under these conditions. The trio lived at Mendips, the name given to the family home on Menlove Avenue in the Liverpool suburb of Woolton. The semidetached, four-bedroom stucco home was comfortable, and John was given the bedroom above the front porch. His half-sister said his room "was a real boy's room, as untidy as the rest of the house was immaculately neat. Books were everywhere.... Over his bed was a collection of cut-out skeletons and various monsters he had made."[4]

John and jovial Uncle George quickly formed a father-son-type relationship. George provided John with a reprieve from the strictness of his aunt. But even at a young age, John had a serious side, too. He took a liking to Aunt Mimi's numerous classic novels, spending hours reading them, and soon began doing some writing and drawing of his own. That love of art continued at nearby Dovedale Primary School, where John won many awards for his drawings.

At times, John did struggle to fit in, mostly because he was having difficulty finding an outlet for his creativity. This often caused him to rebel against authority. By this time, John's mother was sporadically

John with his mother Julia, in 1949. Although John was close with his mother, he was primarily raised by his Aunt Mimi, his mother's older sister, and her husband George.

STRAWBERRY FIELD

At seven, John was diagnosed as nearsighted and given glasses, which he did not like wearing. After school, he would wander through the neighborhood, one of his favorite play places being a mansion-turned-orphanage named Strawberry Field. John often would stare through the strawberry-colored iron gates at the home's entrance, and he attended a fund-raising carnival there every summer.

Many historians have reported that John's childhood was much like those of the orphans living at Strawberry Field—a life filled with depravity, torment, and struggle. But John said that was not true, and that Mimi and George Smith had saved him from such a life.

stopping by Mendips for short visits, only to leave her son with his aunt and uncle when she returned home to the new family she had created with Bobby Dykins. That family included two daughters: Julia, born in 1947, and Jacqueline, born in 1949.

At first, John did not appear bitter about being the odd child out in his mother's life. He attended Sunday school with his friends at St. Peter's Parish Church and enjoyed doing so. But he soon began acting out. John's outspokenness and ever-expanding dirty vocabulary occasionally got him into trouble at church.

That trouble followed John to Quarry Bank High School, which he began attending in 1952. Even the corporal punishment administered by the teachers at the all-boys school did not stop John from misbehaving. He began his first year at Quarry Bank High (which is equivalent to the seventh grade in the United States) as a top student, placed in what was called the "A" class, along with his best friend, Pete Shotton. As the years wore on, Shotton recalled the pair had clowned around and neglected their studies so frequently that they were moved down to the lowest-possible class, the "C" level "among the hardcore troublemakers, deadbeats, and halfwits."[5]

It was not one specific incident that turned John from a top scholar to a "deadbeat" or a "halfwit," rather it was a combination of events. A major part of John's problem, according to Shotton and other biographers, was the inability of the school's instructors to adapt their teaching to individual students. Everyone at Quarry Bank was forced to learn the same material in the same manner, whether that worked for the student or not. John's often-obscene art and writings were overlooked or ridiculed by his teachers, because they did not fit in with what

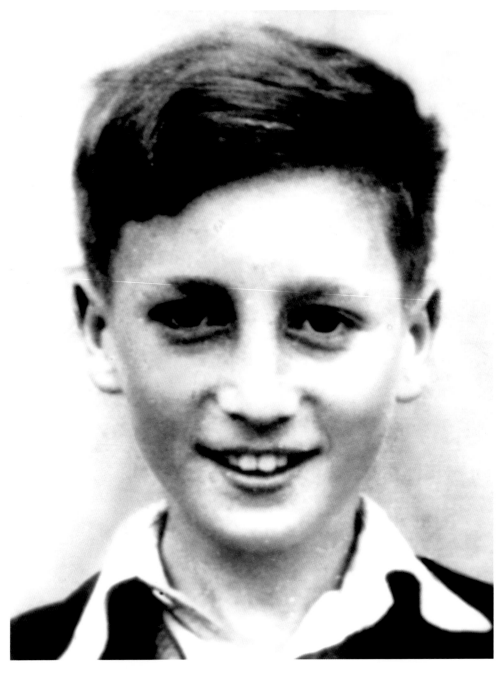

As a child, John was interested in art and music, and his mother Julia encouraged his love of the arts, playing music and singing with her son whenever the two were together.

ELVIS PRESLEY

Elvis Presley had quickly become John's idol. He soaked up all the music he could get his hands on from the barely twenty-year-old Mississippi native. Though Presley's music was heavily influenced by the rhythm and blues black people had been playing for years, the sounds on his records were new to most white audiences, including most everyone in England. John even began imitating his newfound idol, wearing tight pants and sweeping his hair back from his forehead, all the while playing air guitar.

others were doing. John did not let it discourage him. Art remained John's favorite subject, and he would draw whenever he could.

When his Uncle George suddenly died from a liver hemorrhage in 1955, John was profoundly impacted. Another father figure was gone from his life, this one the only adult male confidant he ever had known.

The death left John and his aunt Mimi home alone, save for the boarders his aunt was forced to take in to help pay the bills. Now fourteen, John began neglecting his studies and became a huge burden to his worried aunt. He also began to visit his mother more. As he grew into his teens, he found they had several things in common. He realized his mom was, in many ways, just a big kid.

Songs in the Key of Life

Mother-son tomfoolery was common when the pair were together. Humor and music helped form a bond between the two that time had not been able to. When John visited, his mother always was singing to the songs blasting out of the speakers wired from her record player into every room. Discovering music in the mid-1950s was nowhere near as easy as it is today. There were no computers or smartphones that granted access to thousands of new artists with the click of a mouse or the touch of a screen. Back then, there were only records and the radio, and both had huge impacts on John's life. The records came from John's mom and his pals. The radio came from Radio Luxembourg, a broadcast originating in Belgium that John religiously listened to late at night. The program was dedicated to playing the current American hit songs. To a fifteen-year-old creative English boy looking for an outlet for his rebellious tendencies, the sound coming through his speakers was a shot of pure heaven. The programming he had been able to hear on his country's popular BBC network had been unexciting and family-oriented, not something that would appeal to an unruly teen.

The songs John was listening to were the beginnings of a musical style that would grow to dominate the charts, and it would regularly change the lives of those who listened to it. It was Bill Haley's "Rock Around the Clock," an up-tempo track filled with fast guitar licks, saxophone solos, and bluesy bass lines believed by many to be the first mainstream rock and roll record. It was Presley's cover of black blues singer Arthur Crudup's "That's All Right," and Buddy Holly's "That'll Be the Day." John believed rock and roll changed his life. He said, "[I]t was the only thing to get through to me after all the things that were happening to me when I was fifteen."[6]

John looked the part of a rock-and-roller, but he was a long ways from actually becoming one. He had been playing harmonica since he was in elementary school, and had been known to have a decent musical ear, just as his mother and father had, but he never had performed on a serious level.

All the musicians John listened to as a kid came from America because no Englishmen at the time were playing rock and roll. That changed in 1956, when British musicians such as Tommy Steele began copying the American stars, and some, most notably Lonnie Donegan, began making the style their own.

Donegan, a native of Glasgow, Scotland, pioneered a style of music called "skiffle," in which musicians used nontraditional instruments such as washboards, jugs, and other items to make their music. It was an adaptation of an American musical genre called "rockabilly." In his skiffle band, Donegan played acoustic guitar and sang, and his style of playing affected thousands of British kids once he became popular. His cover of black blues guitarist Leadbelly's "Rock Island Line" debuted on the charts in 1956, and from there it was full steam ahead on the skiffle craze. Skiffle bands popped up across England, and Liverpool had more than its share of them. John wanted to start a skiffle band, too, but he had one big problem: He did not play the guitar. He set out to change that.

John called upon his mother, who taught John how to pick several of his favorite hit songs on the banjo. But what John really wanted was an acoustic guitar like Donegan and Presley. After many days of prayer—and many more staring in the windows of stores and at the guitar ads in magazines—John's wish was granted.

The story of how John got his first guitar has varied through the years. Some historians believe it came from his Aunt Mimi, who finally relented to her nephew's incessant begging. Others believe it was bought by his mother. All report, however, that John's first guitar was a cheap, second-hand model. John did not seem to mind. He took a few lessons but did not like them, and learned some basic banjo chords from his mother, which he translated to the guitar as best he could. The first song he learned to play was "That'll Be the Day." John practiced relentlessly, much to the chagrin of Aunt Mimi, who wished her nephew would spend the time focusing on his studies. At one point, she even told him, "The guitar's all very well, John. But you'll never make a living out of it."[7]

The discouraging words did not faze him, and soon John formed his own band. John later said, "I think the bloke whose idea it was didn't get in the group. We met in his house the first time. There was Eric Griffiths on guitar, Pete Shotton on washboard, Len Garry, Colin Hanton on drums, and Rod [Davis] on banjo."[8] John sang and played guitar, just like Donegan and Presley. John's band members often changed depending on who was available and the band went through various names, too. The group of ambitious and inexperienced teenagers eventually began calling themselves the Quarrymen [sometimes written as two words, Quarry Men], after a line in the official song of Quarry Bank High School. The name stuck, and John now had a band of his own.

2

Becoming the Beatles

The Quarrymen had many musical shortcomings, but the band's enthusiasm helped make up for a lot of them. John was the band's leader from the beginning. On stage, he would strum his cheap guitar with abandon, often breaking a string or two in the middle of a song, yet continuing without missing a beat. None of the band members knew the proper way to play any songs, yet they faked their way through the hottest skiffle tracks from Lonnie Donegan and others, and also sprinkled in some American rock and roll.

John's playing and singing in these early shows stood out, and those who were there have dubbed them memorable. But, like the hundreds of other neighborhood skiffle acts that had popped up in England in the mid-1950s, the Quarrymen almost certainly were sure to fold. But on July 6, 1957, the odds of the Quarrymen being that one-in-a-million success story increased dramatically. On that day, the band was playing a party at St. Peter's Parish Church in Woolton when John's childhood friend, Ivan Vaughan, brought along a schoolmate to introduce to John. This friend was a baby-faced fifteen-year-old named Paul McCartney.

Paul McCartney

James Paul McCartney was born June 18, 1942, at Walton Hospital in Liverpool to working-class parents. His father, Jim, was a lathe turner at Napier's aircraft factory and his mother, Mary, was a nurse who once had worked at Walton Hospital. His parents had waited a long time to marry and even longer to start a family. The pair wed a year before James Paul—who became known by his middle name before he even came home from the hospital—was born, when Jim McCartney was thirty-nine years old and Mary McCartney was thirty-two.

Jim McCartney was an amateur musician with a good ear and often could be found pounding away to the current hit songs on the family piano. Years before Paul was born, Jim had been in a band called the Masked Melody Makers, and he had performed at small venues across Liverpool.

Before Paul was two, his parents gave him his only sibling, Peter Michael, who also went by his middle name. Being a two-income family placed the McCartneys in a good spot financially, but by no means were they rich—or stable. The family was forced to move a lot to accommodate Jim McCartney's job. Paul was a good student and, in 1953, was one of only four kids out of ninety who passed the eleven-plus exam, a requirement to enter a university. His score earned him a spot at the Liverpool Institute, one of the top schools in England. To get to the downtown Liverpool school, Paul had to ride the bus an hour each way every day.

At fourteen, Paul's hour-long bus ride to school each day ended when his family moved closer to the center of Liverpool to a section of town called Allerton. That is where Paul's fascination with American rock and roll began, and also where he first heard Lonnie Donegan's skiffle music.

Rock-and-roll music came into Paul's life around the same time his mother left it. Mary McCartney had long suffered from pains in her breast, and she had a mastectomy when breast cancer was discovered to be the cause. But by that point, the cancer was too far along, and Mary died on October 31, 1956.

Paul turned to music to cope with his mother's death, and he became obsessed with the art form. His discovery of rock and roll made the trumpet his father had given him passé, and now he wanted a guitar like his favorite musicians were playing. He traded his trumpet for one, and played it nonstop, entered school talent shows, and learned the current hits. He even wrote songs, the first being "I Lost My Little Girl."

Paul was a fairly skilled musician by the time he was introduced to John Lennon, at least compared to most fifteen year olds. After the Quarrymen's performance had ended that summer day in 1956, he had the opportunity to show John how good he was. Hearing Paul playing and singing, John quickly realized this, though the egotistical leader in him also was a little intimidated by the younger boy.

Paul actually knew the proper chords to the songs he played, unlike John who only knew the banjo-translated versions. And Paul was singing the correct words, too. Soon, John's ego lost out to Paul's talent. Paul was asked to join the Quarrymen. He accepted, but was leaving on vacation for the rest of the summer, so he did not immediately start practicing with them. Paul's first show

John and his first band, the Quarrymen, performing in July 1957. It was through the Quarrymen that John first met Paul McCartney, and later formed the Beatles.

with the band was a dance at the New Clubmoor Hall in a prosperous section of Liverpool on October 18, 1957.

A New Lineup

"They've been trying to knock us down since we began, especially the British press, always saying, 'What are you going to do when the bubble bursts?' That was the in-crowd joke with us. We'd go when we decided, not when some fickle public decided, because we were not a manufactured group. We knew what we were doing."

John and Paul dressed up for the show, donning cream-colored sport jackets, while the rest of the band wore white shirts with black ties. By all accounts, Paul was less than spectacular during his debut with the Quarrymen. He made several mistakes. But Paul's flubs did not anger John, they actually made him laugh. A long-lasting and successful partnership had begun.

By now, music had become the most-important aspect of John's life, a fact his aunt Mimi loathed. She wanted him to focus on his studies, but John would not budge. So when he failed an important exam, which would have allowed him to continue on at Quarry Bank High School, Aunt Mimi stepped in to do something about it. Failing the test could have meant the end of John's formal education, and Mimi was having none of it. Since John was talented at drawing, as well, Mimi demanded he apply to Liverpool College of Art. He had applied once before but had been rejected. But this time, with Mimi riding him the whole way, he was accepted into the school. For the next four years, studying at the downtown Liverpool school was to be John's full-time job.

Initially, school did shift some of John's focus from his music, but that did not last long. After Paul joined the Quarrymen, the two began spending a lot of time together practicing, playing, and eventually writing their own music. The Quarrymen's lineup began to change. The addition of a fourteen-year-old blue-chip guitarist helped the band change sounds from skiffle to rock and roll.

George Harrison

Harry and Louise Harrison's fourth and final child was born too late to experience the poverty his three older siblings had lived through. By the time George Harold Harrison was born on February 25, 1943, at his home in Liverpool, the Harrisons no longer had to rely on charity to help them get by. A couple of years prior, Harry Harrison had obtained a steady job as a bus driver, one which he kept for thirty-one years.

The big-eared, often-sick George was an entertainer from a young age. He regularly sang along with the tunes playing on his family's gramophone, and he entertained family and friends with his animal puppets.

When George was six, his family moved to a bigger house in Speke, the same Liverpool suburb the McCartney family called home. George enjoyed spending time in the area's natural surroundings, traveling by bicycle or foot to local lakes and ponds. He attended Dovedale Primary School, the same one John Lennon had, and was a decent student. Until he discovered his passion for music.

George's mother bought him his first guitar in 1953. It came from one of his classmates at Dovedale, and was a cheap, small-model instrument that was difficult to keep in tune. Its high-string action also made it difficult to play, especially for a ten year old with small hands. George's fingers bled regularly when he played, and he often became frustrated with his guitar. But he never stopped playing.

At twelve, George passed the eleven-plus exam, allowing him to enter the Liverpool Institute. The semi-exclusive school did not turn out to be a good fit. His teachers were not able to capture his attention the way the guitar could. As was the case with many British teens of the time, it was rock and roll he longed to play, and Elvis Presley was his favorite.

George rode the same bus to school as Paul McCartney did, and the two struck up a friendship. They soon began practicing music together, too, even as Paul was playing and practicing with the Quarrymen. When John first saw George play guitar in early 1958, George, then just fourteen, was asked to join the Quarrymen.

A Musical Evolution

John and Paul spent hours practicing at each other's homes without the rest of their bandmates. John's art school was around the corner from the Liverpool Institute, so the two even got together for lunchtime jam sessions. Their personalities were as different as could be, but when they played music together, they clicked.

Some of their earliest songs, including "One After 909" and "Love Me Do," were good enough to surface on future recordings. The pair also came to an early business agreement: regardless of who had written which part, the team of "Lennon-McCartney" always would be listed as the

JULIA'S LAST MOMENTS

With darkness closing in on the warm evening of July 15, 1958, Julia decided it was time to end her visit at Aunt Mimi's house to return home, where John was waiting to see her. As Julia was about to leave, Nigel Whalley showed up looking for John. When he found he was not there, Nigel offered to walk Julia partway to her bus stop. When they got there, Nigel turned to head to home as Julia crossed Menlove Avenue. She was more than halfway to her destination when Nigel heard the sound of screeching tires. Turning to face the sound, Nigel saw Julia's body fly through the air and crash to the ground, where he rushed to be by her side. Mimi had heard the accident from inside her house and ran outside to attend to her sister. An ambulance arrived a few minutes later and took Julia to the hospital, but it was no use. John's mother was dead. She was only forty-four years old.

song's writers. Though that was not the case in mid-1958, when the Quarrymen recorded for the first time in the home of a man named Percy Phillips. With little money to pay for their recording, the Quarrymen were forced to record their chosen two songs in one take each. They chose Buddy Holly's "That'll Be the Day" as their main song on the record, or the A-side, while the other song, the B-side, was an original tune called "In Spite of All the Danger." When the recording was done, Phillips pressed the music as the band—which now included Lennon, McCartney, Harrison, Colin Hanton, and piano player John "Duff" Lowe—waited. The final product was a flimsy record—though both songs were well done, especially given the circumstance—with song titles handwritten by Phillips. Both sides of the disk read "Recorded by P. F. Phillips," and listed the composers of the respective songs. For "In Spite of All the Danger," on which Lennon sang lead vocals, that credit was given to the team of "McCartney, Harrison." The record later became the most-sought-after record ever produced, worth an estimated $200,000. Unfortunately, John's mother Julia never got to see the heights her son's songwriting partnership eventually would take him to.

Across town, John had noticed his mother was out later than usual. He said, "An hour or so after it happened a copper came to the door to let us know about the accident. It was awful, like some dreadful film where they ask you if you're the victim's son and all that. Well, I was, and I can tell you it was absolutely the worst night of my entire life."[1]

John's mother's death dealt a big behavioral setback to the already-unruly seventeen-year-old. He said, "I

LOVE ME DO

Although his school days were numbered, John still hung out around the Liverpool College of Art, mostly so he could socialize. He had his first serious girlfriend a couple years earlier—a curvy, blonde neighborhood girl named Barbara Baker—but art school is where John's love life fully bloomed. His first college girlfriend was Thelma Pickles, with whom he had a short, often-heated relationship. She said John, still reeling from his mom's death, sometimes would lash out in anger. Thelma's replacement on John's arm was a fellow art school student named Cynthia Powell.

Powell was a year older than Lennon, but the two immediately clicked. Like Lennon, she also had lost a parent when she was young—her dad had died of lung cancer when she was seventeen. She and John met in lettering class. It certainly was not love at first sight, at least not for Powell.

But Powell soon softened and began falling for John once he began showing her more of his sensitive side. He even serenaded her one afternoon with a song he had written called, "Ain't She Sweet." The two began dating, and Cynthia would grow to play an important role in John's life.

lost my mother twice. Once as a child of five and then again at seventeen."[2]

For John, the period following his mother's death was filled with self-destruction. He began drinking regularly and acting out more than ever. He never was a great student, but now he all but gave up on his studies. He even began dressing the part of what was known as a Teddy boy, rebelling against authority with his long jacket, suede shoes, skinny tie, and greased-back hair.

Even the Quarrymen's now-frequent public appearances decreased after the death of John's mother. But John did turn to the guitar for comfort, and continued composing songs with Paul, with whom he now shared a morbid connection. Both boys had lost their mothers. Years later, John sang "a song of love" for his mom on the track "Julia," which was released in 1968. Two years later, he told his mom "good-bye" in the song "Mother."

Stuart Sutcliffe

Born June 23, 1940, in Edinburgh, Scotland, Stuart Fergusson Victor Sutcliffe—like many children born during World War II—was a military child. His father, Charles, was a naval officer frequently away at sea, and his mother, Millie, was a school teacher. When he was three, his family moved to Liverpool, where Stuart began carving a name for himself as an artist. That led to him being accepted into the Liverpool College of Art at the age sixteen.

Sutcliffe's musical ability was as poor as his artistic ability was good, but he loved rock and roll nearly as much as Lennon. The two bonded over songs and art,

After the Quarrymen split up, John and the remaining members, Paul McCartney and George Harrison, formed a new group, the Silver Beatles. Here they are shown performing at a club in 1960.

and formed a deep friendship that arguably became the best Lennon would ever have.

By that time, late 1959, The Quarrymen had dwindled down to just the three guitarists: Lennon, McCartney, and Harrison. The trio briefly flirted with a name change to Johnny and the Moondogs for an audition for a spot on *The Carol Levis Discovery* television show, but quickly realized they needed a drummer and a bassist if they were to keep pace with the current rock and roll outfits. The bass player's spot was filled in November, after Sutcliffe sold one of his paintings and used the proceeds to buy a bass guitar. He had no experience with the instrument, but Lennon welcomed him into his group, regardless.

The band still was without a drummer, thanks to the unpleasant departure of Colin Hanton a short time earlier. The band went through a few short-time replacements, including Tommy Moore, who was in his mid-thirties when he joined the group. Then, in August 1960, Pete Best finally came on to drum with Lennon, McCartney, Harrison, and Sutcliffe.

Pete Best

Randolph Peter Best's background was more diverse—
and his family better off financially—than the other
Quarrymen. Pete, as his family called him, was born
November 24, 1941, in India, where his once-successful
boxing promoter father, John Best, was stationed as a
physical education teacher for the British army. Pete's
mother, Mona, was a Red Cross worker also living in
India, which is where the couple had met.

When World War II ended in 1945, the Best family
left for Britain, ending up in Liverpool, where Pete began
attending school. In his autobiography, Best wrote that
he "went to various schools until I won a scholarship to
Liverpool Collegiate in Shaw Street. By my mid-teens
I had . . . decided that perhaps the teaching profession
was the one for me. I suppose you would describe us as
a middle-class family and teaching somehow fit into that
pattern. That is, until the Casbah came along."[3]

The Casbah did alter the course of Pete's life, and
the lives of countless other Liverpudlians coming of age
in the late-1950s. The Casbah was a rudimentary first
private, then public club located in the expansive cellar of
the Best family home. The Quarrymen were the first band
to play there, on August 29, 1959. They played the club
several more times, and the Casbah's membership grew
as time went on. The club also became a regular hangout
for Lennon and the other band members, even when they
were not playing.

Living at the club left Pete constantly around musicians,
and he soon began to tinker with the drums. His tinkering
evolved into a stint with his first band, The Blackjacks. As
Pete's skills progressed, and Lennon and Co. had begun

yet another search for a permanent drummer, Pete was invited to tryout and won the gig.

After all the personnel changes, and the shift in the band's musical style, the Quarrymen name no longer seemed to fit. Lennon decided it was time for a new name for his band. After a few name changes, the band went with The Silver Beetles then dropped the first word, added an "a" where the second "e" would be, and became the Beatles.

3

Made in Germany

There are countless theories as to how the Beatles got their name. At various times, John Lennon has taken credit for coming up with the name, and George Harrison has given Lennon credit a time or two, as well. Another common theory is that the name was inspired by the name of Buddy Holly's band, the Crickets. But the most-common belief is that the band's new name came from Stuart Sutcliffe. On that subject, Beatles biographer Hunter Davies wrote:

"It had come from that Marlon Brando film, *The Wild One*. There is a group of motorcyclists in the film, all in black leather, called the Beetles, though they are only referred to as such in passing. Stu Stucliffe saw this film, heard the remark, and came back and suggested it to John as the new name for their group. John said yeh, but we'll spell it *Beatles*, as we're a beat group. Well, that's one theory. No doubt, in years to come, there will be new suggestions."[1]

Pete Best officially joined the band shortly after the other four members had returned from a somewhat disastrous tour of Scotland in support of a Liverpool native and Elvis Presley lookalike named Johnny Gentle. Within a few weeks, Best and the rest of the Beatles set off for Hamburg, Germany, for a forty-eight-night residency at the Indra Club. It was a trip that would shape their careers—and lives—for years to come.

When the Beatles arrived in Hamburg in the middle of August 1960, the five young lads discovered a city that was much like their home base of Liverpool. Both were gritty port cities—Hamburg on the Elbe River, Liverpool on the Mersey. Both had been brutalized by bombs during the war, and now had their share of crime and illicit

The original lineup of the Beatles featured, from left: George Harrison, Paul McCartney, Pete Best, and John Lennon.

underground activity. Even so, Hamburg's reputation was by far the worst of the two. The Beatles were thrust into the city's seedy side. The small Indra Club was located inside the basement of a former strip club in the middle of the Hamburg's red-light district, where prostitution and gang combat was commonplace. But Allan Williams, the Liverpool club owner and de facto Beatles manager responsible for booking the band in Hamburg, had been told the city was a great place for bands to play.

Williams eventually would be proven correct, but not at first. In fact, just a handful of people witnessed the first Beatles show at Indra, and those who did were not impressed. The cramped stage the band was sharing used to be where the strippers would dance, and the Germans that frequented the club were used to seeing serious movement from the club's musical performers. The Beatles were a fairly tame bunch. They did not jump around wildly, instead they would calmly sing and play. This was not working for the Indra Club regulars. On subsequent nights, the crowd chanted *Mach Schau* [make show] to the band, signaling they wanted to see some energy. As soon as Lennon and the rest of the Beatles began to *Mach Schau*, the crowds slowly began to grow.

In Hamburg, the Beatles played four and a half hours each weeknight, and six hours on weekends. They played from early in the evening until early the following morning, sometimes seven days a week. The workload forced the band to come up with new material, and they also had to lengthen the songs they already had. It was on-the-job training with the pay coming both in money and beer, the latter which the crowd would literally hand the band members as they performed.

Off stage, the Beatles were housed in cramped quarters in the Bambi Kino, a run-down theater owned by the club's owner, Bruno Koschmider. The quintet lived in three small dressing rooms behind the theater's screen, and they used the urinals for both their intended purpose and to wash themselves.

Hamburg was a city where sexuality was openly talked about and sex acts were openly performed. It was a far cry from Liverpool's more-conservative attitude, and German girls began flocking to the Beatles. This worried Cynthia Powell, John's longtime girlfriend, who was back in Liverpool as her nineteen-year-old steady received numerous propositions from Hamburg's sexually desensitized women.

After numerous noise complaints from someone living above the Indra, Koschmider decided to revert the basement space to a strip club, and he moved the Beatles down the street to the nicer Kaiserkeller club, where they opened for another Liverpool band, Rory Storm and The Hurricanes. Kaiserkeller is where Klaus Voorman first discovered the Beatles, as did his longtime girlfriend, Astrid Kirchherr.

One night as he was walking by the Kaiserkeller, Voorman poked his head into the club to see who was creating the brilliant sounds he could hear from the streets. A few nights later, he and Kirchherr returned to the club. It was a move the young German man soon would regret. The good-looking Kirchherr took an immediate liking to the Beatles—both to their music and to the individuals producing it. Her favorite Beatle was Sutcliffe, and she and the artist-turned-bass player quickly struck up a romantic relationship, leaving Voorman behind.

DRUGS TAKE HOLD

Hamburg was where the Beatles were introduced to something else they had not seen before: the drug Preludin, better known as prellies, a stimulant that was prescribed for weight loss, but also taken for energy. Prellies became a late-night staple in all the Beatles' diets, helping them maintain their vigor and stay awake, even after a long, hard night playing music in a sweaty club. Lennon proved to be particularly vulnerable to the drug. Kirchherr said the prellies allowed John to open up, but that the commonly held belief that the Beatles were always on drugs when they were in Hamburg was not true.

Spending time with Sutcliffe also meant spending time with the other members of the Beatles, and Kirchherr had a big impact on all of them. She trimmed their hair into a style closely resembling her own—a forward-combed, bowl-shaped style that the Beatles eventually would become famous for. The twenty-two-year-old Kirchherr, along with her friend Jurgen Vollmer, also photographed the band several times, the first photographer to do so seriously.

The band's stay in Hamburg was extended thanks to their success, and in late October the Beatles were offered the chance to move from the Kaiserkeller to the new Top Ten Club. But soon after, the police were tipped off to the fact that George Harrison was only seventeen, and he had

Although drummer Pete Best was a founding member of the group, he would be replaced by Ringo Starr before the band hit it big, being fired from the group in 1962.

no working permit that would allow him to legally be in Germany. He was not even old enough to be in the clubs he had been playing in since August. George was given twenty-four hours to leave the country, and he had to take a train back to Liverpool.

The day after George left, a mischievous McCartney and Best set a small fire at the Bambi Kino. Though it did no damage, the two were arrested for attempted arson, and they also were found to have no working permits to be in Germany and were deported back to England. Defeated and now without bandmates, Lennon returned

45

to England on his own, while Sutcliffe—who now was engaged to Kirchherr—stayed behind in Hamburg.

Home Sweet Home

Lennon arrived back at Mendips in the middle of the night, defeated, dejected, and depressed. The house was shuttered for the evening, so Lennon had to throw rocks at Aunt Mimi's window to wake her. Mimi, who had warned her nephew against going to Germany at the expense of his studies, was not happy to see Lennon. She wanted to know where all the money was he had told her he was going to make. Lennon ignored his aunt and headed up to his old room above the front porch. For a while before he left for Germany, Lennon had been sharing an apartment with Sutcliffe near Liverpool Art College. But now, feeling defeated, he was back at Mendips, under the watchful eye of his strict aunt.

Lennon laid low for a while. Some accounts say he did not leave Mendips for more than a week. Cynthia Powell said Lennon was excited to see her, that he called as soon as he returned, and he took her to buy a leather jacket with the money he had made in Hamburg. Whatever he did, Lennon did not see any of the other Beatles for a couple weeks, and he often thought about how the band might be finished. For a period, it looked like that might be the case. While Lennon was sulking, a couple of the Beatles had gotten jobs, including Harrison, who mistakenly believed his bandmates still were in Germany.

The Beatles reformed within a few weeks, and started playing in Liverpool. The first comeback show happened December 17 at the Casbah. Show posters advertising the gig were plastered across town. With Sutcliffe still in

Hamburg, Chas Newby, a member of Pete Best's former group, The Blackjacks, played bass. Ten days later, a disc jockey named Bob Wooler helped the Beatles get another gig at the Litherland Town Hall. Those in attendance hardly knew of the Beatles, but from the opening riff of the first song, Little Richard's raucous "Long Tall Sally," the crowd was mesmerized. Instead of socializing in their

The Beatles, with friend Tony Sheridan, perform onstage in Hamburg, Germany, during one of the band's first tours out of England in the early 1960s.

own little groups as they did for most bands' performances, the club-goers rushed to the stage to feed off the energy the band members were exuding with their own dancing and head-bobbing.

Beatles scholars have since recognized that night, December 27, 1960, as a major turning point. Lennon himself said, "It was that evening that we really came out of our shell and let go. We discovered we were quite famous."[2]

CLUB NIGHTS, CLUB FIGHTS

Beatles' songs often would energize the crowd so much that fights would break out. Sutcliffe was badly beaten during one of them on January 30, 1961. As he was loading equipment after a show at Lathom Hall in Liverpool, he was attacked by a group of men, who kicked and punched him so many times that he was a bloody mess by the time someone else showed up to fend off the bullies. At various times, other band members were beaten up, as well, and sometimes they would even fight one another. A few months after he was first beaten, Sutcliffe was whipped until he bled by the man he most admired, John Lennon. Lennon, drunk at the time, was upset over some band-related issues and took it out on Sutcliffe.

With the assistance of Brian Kelly and other music promoters, the Beatles—with Stuart Sutcliffe now back from Germany and again on bass—began playing out in many other Liverpool clubs. At Litherland, they were billed every Thursday as "The Magnificent Beatles!! John, Paul, George and Pete."[3] Sutcliffe was not named.

The Beatles also played at the Cavern Club, the jazz joint where the Quarrymen had once played to little success. But musical trends had changed since that time, and the old warehouse was now a happening rock-and-roll hangout soon to become the Beatles' home away from home. During the next two years, the band played there nearly three hundred times. Many of those shows came during lunchtime, when Lennon would have been in art school, had he not dropped out prior to his first trip to Germany.

Meanwhile, Lennon became frustrated with Sutcliffe, a feeling shared by McCartney and Harrison. Both men had been pressuring Lennon to toss his friend out because his musical ability—as Sutcliffe himself was well aware—was not up to par with the other members, and also because his focus was shifting from music back to painting.

Sutcliffe's altercation with Lennon occurred in Hamburg, where the Beatles had returned to in April 1961 for another tour. Sutcliffe quit the band while they were there, leaving the Beatles in a desperate situation. Who was going to play bass? Lennon and Harrison refused to give up their guitars, so McCartney agreed to. He bought a violin-shaped bass and took over Sutcliffe's four-string duties.

In June, the Beatles were asked to perform as the backup band for singer Tony Sheridan at a recording session at a local school. They agreed, and recorded seven songs. One of them, "My Bonnie," was released as a single later that year on Polydor Records, and it did mildly well in Germany. It was released in that country as coming from Sheridan and "The Beat Brothers," which the producer had insisted the Beatles be called. That producer, popular German musician Bert Kaempfert, was impressed by "The Beat Brothers," and signed them to a one-year contract with Polydor. Kaempfert also allowed the Beatles to record two of their own songs that day, an instrumental called "Cry for a Shadow," and a version of the jazz song "Ain't She Sweet," featuring Lennon on lead vocals. Neither of those songs was released, but the recording session did go down in history as being the Beatles' first.

When they returned to England in July, the Beatles resumed their performances at the Cavern Club. That month also saw the launch of *Mersey Beat*, a local newspaper focusing on the Liverpool music scene. The publication was founded by Bill Harry, a friend of Lennon's from Liverpool Art College. Harry allowed Lennon to write an article on the history of the Beatles for the paper's first edition. It published July 6, 1961, under the headline: "BEING A SHORT DIVERSION ON THE DUBIOUS ORIGINS OF BEATLES." Lennon's writing, which ran on the front page, provided a tongue-in-cheek biographical sketch of the band.

Mersey Beat became popular in Liverpool, and it featured several more articles on the Beatles, including one announcing that they had signed a recording contract with Polydor. The newspapers were sold across the city, including at the North End Music Stores run by twenty-seven-year-old Brian Epstein. Born into a well-off Jewish family, Epstein began his career managing a small record section in his family's furniture stores. Shortly after *Mersey Beat* began, Epstein began contributing a column to each issue, focusing on new releases at his record store.

A New Leader

Though "My Bonnie" had done nothing on the English charts, people still came into Epstein's shop looking for a copy of it. Epstein said that is how he came to hear about the Beatles, and legend says a record buyer named Raymond Jones was the one who asked for it. Some Beatles historians doubt Epstein's story, saying he surely must have at least heard about the Beatles prior to Jones's trip to his store. Especially considering all the coverage the band was receiving in *Mersey Beat* and the airplay "My Bonnie" was beginning to get on Liverpool radio.

Regardless of how he came to learn of the band, Epstein decided it was time for him to see for himself what all the hoopla surrounding the Beatles was about. On November 9, 1961, the sharp-dressed businessman showed up at the Cavern Club and stuck his nose in the door. He liked what he saw, which shaped the Beatles' career, and in turn, the future of the entire music industry.

Epstein watched the band several more times before inviting them to his office, which he did in December. That is when he offered to be their manager. The band members had their concerns, most notably, would they still be able to play the same music? Epstein assured them they would. The band agreed to let Epstein manage them, and he immediately set to work. He cleaned up their image and turned them into professional musicians, stressing punctuality—which they never had been good at—and focusing their attention on the music.

John Lennon (far left) plays his guitar for his bandmates and manager while the five men relax in a hotel room in Paris during a tour stop.

Almost immediately, Epstein set off to get the Beatles out of their contract with Polydor, which he did, and find the band a new recording contract. On the first day of 1962, he had the boys in London at an audition for Decca Records, but Decca passed. The Decca rejection was not the only one the Beatles would face, but Epstein remained determined. He believed he was onto something, and continued his search for a deal.

Meanwhile, Epstein sent the Beatles back to Germany to play a series of shows at Hamburg's new Star-Club. Rather than driving there in a crammed van as they had on their previous trips to Germany, the Beatles flew to Germany this go-round. The band—minus Harrison, who came a day later—arrived at the Hamburg airport on April 11, and were greeted there by their friend Astrid Kirchherr. Lennon was happy to see her, but there was no smile on the young woman's face and her voice was absent her typical enthusiasm. He knew something was wrong. Kirchherr said, "Stuart's died, John. He's gone."[4]

Lennon burst with laughter. Kirchherr said, "It was frightening. John was laughing but also kind of crying, saying 'No, no, no!' and lashing out with his hands."[5] Lennon's seemingly insensitive display was not out of character, nor did it mean he did not care for Sutcliffe. Many historians have written about how Lennon loved the twenty-one-year-old Sutcliffe like a brother. For evidence, they point to the fact that when Sutcliffe had remained behind in Germany, effectively ending his stint with the Beatles, Lennon began hand-writing him letters filled with heartfelt poetry, drawings, and soul-bearing words.

Sutcliffe had died April 10, a day before the Beatles entered the country. He had been having terrible headaches for months, and officially died from a brain hemorrhage. An autopsy revealed a small indentation in the front of Sutcliffe's skull, which likely had been caused by a major blow to the head. Exactly what that blow was from will never be known, but one theory is that it happened during the beating he had taken more than a year earlier outside Lathom Hall. Some historians have even suggested that the damage to Sutcliffe's skull could have been caused by the beating Lennon had given him in Hamburg.

The distraught band members pulled themselves together after hearing of Sutcliffe's death, and they decided to carry on with their shows. And like most of the Beatles' gigs in Hamburg, they were wild ones. The now-legendary stories from that tour include one where a drunken Lennon took the stage with a toilet seat around his neck, several fighting stories, and another incident where Lennon urinated over the edge of a hotel balcony.

At the time, the stories were nowhere near legendary, because no one outside of a few select areas cared—or even had heard—of John Lennon, Paul McCartney, George Harrison, Pete Best, or their band. Shortly after the band's third trip to Hamburg, that all changed forever.

4

Beatlemania Spreads

While the Beatles were in Hamburg, Brian Epstein remained in England to search for a record deal. He was not having much luck. He still believed in the band's potential, but he also had spent a lot of his own money promoting them, and he appeared ready to give up. With the band's music in his hand, he took a trip to London to give it one final shot. Oddly, it was a trip to a record store there that helped change his fortunes.

Epstein stopped by the store to make some more copies of the demos he was hawking. One of the store's employees liked the recordings, and hooked Epstein up with a friend of his at Parlophone Records, a subsidiary of the gigantic EMI corporation. That friend, George Martin, was head of Parlophone and agreed to give the Beatles an audition.

That audition took place June 6, 1962, at EMI's Abbey Road Studios in London. Four songs were recorded that day, including three originals: "Ask Me Why," "Love Me Do," and "P.S. I Love You." Martin appeared impressed by both the songs and the band members. Everyone that is, except Pete Best. Martin felt his drumming was not up to par. After the tryout, Martin took Epstein aside and told him Best would have to go. After a few short-timers joined the band, Best's replacement was the drummer for Rory Storm and The Hurricanes, Ringo Starr.

Ringo Starr

He was not born a "Starr," or for that matter a "Ringo." His real name was Richard Starkey, and he was born July 7, 1940, in Liverpool, to Richard and Elsie Starkey. Ritchie, as the boy was known, was raised in a rough area of Liverpool called Dingle, the same section of the city where many of his ancestors had spent their entire lives. His parents had met a few years prior in a bakery where they both worked. When Ritchie was three years old, his parents separated, leaving him and his mother alone. His father remained absent most of his childhood. Minus a second income, Ritchie's mother struggled to pay the bills, and she received government aid to help with necessities.

Ritchie was a sickly child, one whose frequent hospital stays seriously affected his education. As a teen he fell so far behind in school, that his only option was to quit and get a job. He tried several, but nothing seemed to stick for long until his stepfather secured him a job as an apprentice at an engineering firm.

The American rock-and-roll craze that had affected so many British youth in the mid-1950s hit Ritchie as well, as did the skiffle craze fueled by the genre's ringleader, Lonnie Donegan. In 1957, Ritchie began his own skiffle group called The Eddie Clayton Skiffle Group. He began by playing rhythm on a skiffle board, and soon his stepfather bought him a secondhand set of drums. When he was eighteen, he moved on to a band called The Raving Texans, which soon morphed into Rory Storm and The Hurricanes. He was with that outfit when he took on the stage name he forever would be known by, Ringo Starr. His time with Rory Storm and The Hurricanes also helped introduce him to the Beatles when the two Liverpool bands played together in 1960 at the Kaiserkeller club in Hamburg.

The Beginning of Something New

With his band's permanent—and final—lineup in place, and a recording contract signed, it seemed natural that

John and his first wife Cynthia together on the plane to New York for the Beatles' first tour of the United States in 1964. The couple married in 1962, shortly after the Beatles signed their first contract.

58

Lennon would have to focus most of his attention on the Beatles. But domestic matters actually took precedence during this time of his life when he discovered that his girlfriend was pregnant, and he was going to be a father. A few weeks later, on August 23, 1962, he and Cynthia Powell went down to the Mount Pleasant Registry Office in Liverpool, and wed in a short ceremony. No members of Lennon's family attended, not even his aunt Mimi.

The newlyweds made their home in an apartment owned by Epstein, which he let them use for free as a wedding gift. Despite his rough demeanor, Lennon received high marks from his wife. Outside his house, Lennon's marriage was kept under wraps so female fans would continue clamoring to win his affection during his shows.

With Best out and Starr in behind the drum kit, the Beatles returned to Abbey Road Studios in September to make their first record for Parlophone. The foursome's takes included a simple number called "Love Me Do," which featured Lennon on harmonica, and another track, "P.S. I Love You." The following month, "Love Me Do" was released to the public as the Beatles' first single.

The "Love Me Do" single, which featured "P.S. I Love You" as its B-side, sold well in the Beatles' hometown of Liverpool, where they already were popular. The song even found its way onto England's record charts, peaking at number seventeen, a big accomplishment for a new band. The Beatles also were excited to hear themselves on Radio Luxembourg, the Belgian rock and roll broadcast Lennon said had changed his life when he was a teenager. Shortly thereafter, the Beatles performed on radio and TV programs, and opened two shows for Little Richard, one of the popular American rock and roll singers who originally had helped inspire them to become musicians.

On November 26, the band returned to Abbey Road Studios to record again, this time choosing a song Lennon originally had written as a ballad. It was called "Please Please Me." But Martin was not interested in a slow song as the band's second single, so the Beatles reworked it, turning it into an all-out rocker clocking in at slightly more than two minutes long. When the band finished recording the song, Martin was ecstatic. "Please Please Me" was released in January 1963, and rose up the charts, buoyed by a performance of the song on the national television show, *Thank Your Lucky Stars*. The song eventually topped out at number two.

The Beatles at Abbey Road recording studio, signing paperwork for their single "She Loves You," which was recorded at Abbey Road and released in 1963.

Shortly after, the Beatles set out on their first major tour of Britain, playing venues large and small. At each stop, girls would scream wildly for the band, and opening for them was difficult.

The Beatles entered the recording studio for an eleven-hour session in the middle of February to record an album. The final product was called *Please Please Me*, after the successful single of the same name, and it was released in Britain on March 22. The album featured fourteen songs—eight Lennon-McCartney originals and six covers. It began with the energetic rocker "I Saw Her Standing There" and ended roughly thirty minutes later in complete chaos with a hoarse Lennon screaming the lyrics to a song initially made popular by The Isley Brothers, "Twist and Shout." The song was recorded in one take.

After their recording session, the Beatles returned to the road and continued their rigorous promotional

JULIAN LENNON

John Charles Julian Lennon was three days old before his father made it to the hospital to see him. Forever to be known as Julian, a derivative of his late grandmother's name, Julia, the Lennons' first child had been born early in the morning on April 8. A few days later, the famous rocker was back on tour, pretending to be a bachelor, with a baby and a lonely wife at home.

schedule. They even came back to Abbey Road in early March to record their next single. This one, released in April, was called "From Me to You." It was recorded the same month Lennon would return home from tour to discover some life-changing news.

Cynthia Lennon's pregnancy had been a difficult one filled with loneliness and complicated by health scares. She was so lonely, that she had moved in with John's aunt Mimi so she would have some company during the last stages of her pregnancy.

Cynthia now accepted having her husband away from home so frequently. That did not mean she enjoyed it, especially with a new baby to take care of, but she understood his need to tour. It was how he supported his family. She had been raised in an era where men were absent from the home all the time, away at sea for work or off fighting for their country in World War II.

Cynthia even was supportive when her husband asked her if he could go on vacation to Spain with Epstein, less than three weeks after Julian was born. The Beatles were on a rare break from their rigorous work schedule, and Cynthia said John could go. John may not have had the issues of being famous to deal with in Spain, but the trip still managed to create controversy in their lives.

Although he never told anyone but his closest friends, it was common knowledge that Epstein was a homosexual, which, at the time, was illegal in England. Lennon knew this, and often had made jokes about it both in and out of Epstein's presence. Neither man seemed to care.

But when word got out that Lennon and Epstein had gone on vacation alone together, rumors spread that Lennon also was gay and that he and Epstein were having an affair. Lennon even got into a bloody fight with disc jockey Bob Wooler when Wooler teased him about his relationship with Epstein. Many historians believe some sort of physical intimacy did occur between the two men on their trip, though exactly what has never been determined.

In April 1963, John became a father for the first time when Cynthia gave birth to their son, Julian. Julian was immortalized in the Beatles song "Hey Jude," which was written for him by Paul McCartney.

COVERS

As the Beatles' popularity grew, other bands began covering their songs. One group that did so was The Rolling Stones, who went on to become a worldwide smash. The Beatles had allowed the Stones—led by energetic singer Mick Jagger, guitarist Keith Richards, and multi-instrumentalist Brian Woods—to record a song considered to be a throwaway, "I Wanna Be Your Man." It was not a throwaway for the Stones—their version of the fairly unpopular (at least by Beatles standards) tune reached number twelve on the British charts.

Straight to the Top

Even controversies such as this could not bring the Beatles down. A fourth single recorded at Abbey Road, "She Loves You," shot straight to number one. The band appeared on radio and television nearly nonstop, and the four members were becoming household names in Britain. Even those who were not rock and roll fans knew who the Beatles were. In large part, that was due to the Beatles' performance before Queen Elizabeth II on November 4 during the *Royal Variety Show*.

Even in front of the stuffy crowd at the Prince of Wales Theatre in London, the Beatles were their usual playful selves, especially the sarcastic Lennon.

Fans began showing up at the band members' homes, often making for some scary situations. For example, prior to the Beatles' appearance on the extremely popular Val Parnell's *Sunday Night at the London Palladium* TV show, a group of fans lined up outside the studio hoping to get a glimpse of the band. When the band members came out of rehearsal, screaming fans swarmed their car, blocking the path from the building. The band members rushed to the car and dove inside, as fans tried to grab them. After the show, there were two thousand fans outside. The next day, photos of the scene were plastered in every newspaper in London. *The Daily Mirror* featured two photos of girls in various states of hysteria, the larger photo showing a girl screaming with her hands on her head, held back by the hands of a security guard. The one-word exclamatory headline at the top of the page succinctly summed up what was happing to Britain: Beatlemania!

While rock star John Lennon was being accosted by fans, staying in luxury hotels in London and worshipped by thousands, his wife and his child were leading a much different life back in Liverpool, living in a rented room with Cynthia's mother and keeping the marriage as secret as possible.

Her loyalty eventually was rewarded, and in January 1964, she, John, and Julian moved into a three-bedroom apartment in London. She was happy her family finally was living together, but she was not happy with the lack of privacy in their new home. Once fans figured out where they lived, they began to pester the Lennons, even camping outside their apartment waiting for someone to come outside. By that time, the Beatles' second album, *With the Beatles*, had been released to overwhelming praise. The album, a lot less raw than the Beatles' first full-length, featured eight original tracks, including "Don't Bother Me" written by Harrison, "All My Loving," and the song the band had allowed The Rolling Stones to release, "I Wanna Be Your Man." The album did not include their fifth single, the peppy "I Want to Hold Your Hand," which was released a few days later.

> **"I'm always proud and pleased when people do my songs. It gives me pleasure that they even attempt them, because a lot of my songs aren't that doable."**

Had they moved across the Atlantic Ocean to America, the Lennons easily could have lived in anonymity anywhere they desired. Popularity in the United States still eluded the band, even after a deal with Vee-Jay Records allowed their records to be released there. "Please Please Me" was the first US release, and it did not do well. In fact, the Beatles were such nobodies that initial pressings of the single misspelled the name of the band as the "Beattles."

Detailed plans were in the works to change that. Epstein flew to New York in November for several meetings to prepare for the Beatles' first visit to the United States. The visit was scheduled for February 1964, and the band was to perform on the popular *Ed Sullivan Show*. At the time, an appearance on the show meant everything to an act, and easily could make—or break—it. Epstein had arranged for the Beatles to play the show twice. He also booked a show for them at New York City's prestigious Carnegie Hall. An answer to whether US audiences would embrace the Beatles would certainly come in a few months. But, as it turns out, the band did not have to wait quite that long to find out.

Beatlemania Crosses the Atlantic

In mid-January, "I Want to Hold Your Hand" entered the top one hundred on the US singles charts. Copies of the record flew off store shelves, eventually selling more than five million copies in the United States alone. During the first week of February, "I Want to Hold Your Hand" hit number one, and stayed there for seven weeks, until it was knocked off by another Beatles song, "She Loves You."

By that time, the band was already on its way to the States. The promotional machine had beaten them there, plastering word of the Beatles' impending arrival across the country. Both *Time* and *Life* magazines had written about them, and their back catalog of songs was being spun nonstop on radio stations. The frenzy that surrounded the band when they first touched down on American soil on February 7, 1964, was unexpected by some, though it should not have been.

Seventy-three million people tuned in on February 9 to watch the Beatles on *The Ed Sullivan Show* on CBS. It was the most-watched TV program in American history. Significantly fewer people, slightly more than seven hundred, were in the audience to see it live. The Beatles played five songs: "All My Loving," "Till There Was You," "She Loves You," "I Saw Her Standing There," and the chart-topping "I Want to Hold Your Hand." Listeners were treated to an extra, somewhat unexpected, instrument on each song—the chorused screams of the hundreds of young girls in the studio. The band had also taped a second performance earlier that day, which was broadcast on the show two weeks later.

The excitement carried over to the Beatles' first American concert, held two days later at the Coliseum in Washington, D.C., and the following day during two short concerts at Carnegie Hall in New York City.

The Beatles returned to England at the end of the month, and in March they began production on their first movie, *A Hard Day's Night*. Band members played themselves in the film, the plot of which revolved around what a typical day in the band's life was fancied to be like—trying to avoid screaming fans while staying out of trouble. Beatles' songs played throughout the film, which premiered in London on July 6. It was a box-office smash,

The Beatles receive gold records, commemorating sales of one million records, for their single "I Want to Hold Your Hand" and their full-length album *Meet the Beatles*.

and also well-reviewed by critics. A music album with the same title as the film was released that summer, as well. Featuring number one singles "A Hard Day's Night" and "Can't Buy Me Love," the record shot straight to the top of the charts and stayed there for several weeks. The latter track sold a world record 2.7 million copies before it was even released.

Anything the Beatles were involved in was an instantaneous smash. That included Lennon's first book, which was published in March 1964. Called *In His Own Write*, the book included several of the author's stories, poems, and drawings. Lennon also wrote *A Spaniard in the Works*, which was published a year later. Both were best sellers.

The Price of Fame

Lennon's fame continued to impact his personal life. One good way was that he now had enough money to do almost anything he desired, including buying a home south of London in the town of Weybridge. The home was a gigantic Tudor mansion called Kenwood, equipped with more than twenty rooms and a swimming pool. The location offered some privacy for his family, who by then had been constantly besieged by fans at their apartment. Shortly, Harrison and his girlfriend, Patti Boyd, and Starr and his girlfriend, Maureen, moved into homes near the Lennons.

Lennon's popularity also sparked a reunion with his long-absent father, Alf. John had not seen his father since he was five years old—roughly twenty years now—and harbored much hatred toward his pop for having abandoned him. As the legend goes, Alf Lennon was working as a dishwasher when one of his coworkers saw a picture of John in a newspaper and pointed it out. That soon led to father and son reuniting on a movie set, where John was filming. According to biographer Bob Spitz, Alf said that he "stuck out my hand to shake his but John just growled at me and said suspiciously, 'What do you want?'"[1] John later said that was because "[h]e turned up after I was famous. . . . He knew where I was all my life—I'd lived in the same house in the same place for most of my childhood, and he knew where."[2]

The next year, Alf Lennon tried to capitalize on the success of his famous son, and released an album under the name "Freddie Lennon." His first single, "That's My Life," was a flop, and his professional music career ended almost as quickly as it had begun. Father and son did not speak again until just days before Alf Lennon died of stomach cancer in 1976.

Another negative byproduct of Lennon's wealth was that he now could afford whatever drugs he wanted. He and the other Beatles had long been users of marijuana, but he now began regularly using LSD. The illegal hallucinogenic, also known as acid, impacted nearly every aspect of Lennon's life. Eventually, it would affect his relationship with his family, his bandmates, and the type of music he created, but for now it was just another way for him to escape the rigors of being a star.

Mass-Produced Madness

In August, the Beatles returned to the United States for their first cross-country tour, beginning in San Francisco on August 19, and ending in New York on September 20. Beatlemania was out in full force on this tour. Because of this, the Beatles kept mostly to their hotel rooms when they were not playing. Even that did not stop creative, and often crazed, fans from attempting to get their hands on the band members. In one instance, on the third stop of the tour on August 21 in Seattle, two girls were found hiding under a bed in the Beatles' hotel.[3]

The Beatles capitalized on their fame by releasing products at a pace that today is nearly unheard of. Their second movie, *Help!,* premiered in August 1965, its plot centered around a religious cult trying to retrieve a special ring that has wound up on Starr's finger. *The Help!* album came out the same month, and it included several songs that had appeared in the film. The record's highlights included the title song, as well as "Ticket to Ride" and "You've Got to Hide Your Love Away," a song written by Lennon in a style inspired by American singer-songwriter Bob Dylan. Lennon and the rest of the Beatles had met Dylan on a previous trip to the United States, and Dylan's folkish, personal lyrics had a great impact on Lennon. Until then, the stories Lennon had told through his songs were semi-vague and chiefly impersonal, but Dylan's influence helped change that. Through Dylan, Lennon discovered that lyrics can be deep and meaningful. With that revelation, his musical direction changed.

The Dylan influence is evident on *Rubber Soul,* which the Beatles released at the end of 1965. Much of the happy "she loves you" lyrics the Beatles had become known for were missing from the album, replaced by darker pieces such as "Norwegian Wood" and "Nowhere Man." Lennon's newfound introspection began to take its toll on the band, however, and a rift between Lennon and songwriting partner McCartney began to develop.

5

"More Popular Than Jesus"

C omments John Lennon made to an English news-paper in the summer of 1966 proved Beatlemania, though strong, was not invincible.

"Christianity will go," Lennon said. "It will vanish and sink. I needn't argue about that. I'm right and will be proved right. We're more popular than Jesus now. I don't know which will go first—rock 'n' roll or Christianity. Jesus was all right, but his disciples were thick and ordinary. It's them twisting it that ruins it for me."[1]

The lengthy article ran in the *London Evening Standard*, and it was reprinted in others, without ill effects. But when portions of the interview were reprinted out of context in an American teen magazine, it was another story. The magazine, *Datebook*, highlighted the "more popular than Jesus" portion of Lennon's quote, which set off a chain reaction of anti-Beatles movements across the United States—especially in the Southern Bible Belt—and in other countries, such as South Africa and Spain. Radio stations everywhere stopped playing Beatles records. Groups gathered to burn their records, pictures, and other memorabilia. Numerous death threats were made against Lennon, and the rest of the Beatles, too. Saying he stood behind what he said, Lennon would not apologize until Brian Epstein finally talked him into it.

The controversy began just as the Beatles were about to begin another US tour. The band was as popular as ever, their latest release *Revolver*—with its key songs "Taxman," "Eleanor Rigby," "Got to Get You Into My Life," and "Yellow Submarine"—again topping the charts. But the tour was almost canceled because of Lennon's comments. As the band traveled across the country, signs reading "Go Home Beatles" and worse followed them, as did some death threats. By the end of the tour, the Beatles were exhausted. After the final show on August 29, 1966, in San Francisco, the band decided they were through touring. The excitement and fun they had in the beginning—playing dives in Hamburg and in Liverpool—had vanished.

The Beatles Take a Break

When they returned to England, the band members went their separate ways. Harrison and his now-wife, Patti, visited India, and explored the religion of that country. McCartney traveled as well, and he took on various other music projects. Starr and his new wife, Maureen, settled into a quiet life at home.

Lennon was unsure of what to do with his time. He accepted a role in the antiwar film, *How I Won the War*, traveling to Spain to film it. He chopped off his hair and donned wire-rimmed glasses to play the role of Private Gripweed. The short haircut did not stick with him long, but Lennon did like the rounded glasses, and they eventually became his trademark.

The Beatles, now with Ringo Starr (left) as the permanent drummer, hold a press conference in Washington, DC, before an August 1966 performance.

When filming was through, Lennon returned to England and became more involved in London's art scene, a move that would change his life as well as the lives of many others. On November 9, he traveled with a friend to the Indica Gallery to see an exhibition titled "Yoko at Indica." Lennon thought the description of the show sounded interesting. His friend had told him it was "about this Japanese girl from New York, who was going to be in a bag, doing this event or happening."[2] The "Japanese girl" was Yoko Ono, a twice-divorced mother of one, avant-garde artist who was seven years Lennon's senior. A short time later, Ono sent Lennon a copy of a book of poetry she had written, *Grapefruit: A Book of Instructions and Drawings*. She also began sending him letters and postcards, and she even visited John and Cynthia's home in Weybridge.

JOHN AND YOKO

During their night spent together, John and Yoko had recorded some strange experimental music, which was released the following year under the title *Unfinished Music No. 1: Two Virgins*. The record was panned by critics and fans alike, and it was most noteworthy for its cover, which featured a black-and-white photograph of Lennon and Ono posing together nude. In 1969, the couple released *Unfinished Music No. 2: Life with the Lions*. It, too, failed to garner the kind of attention and praise that Lennon's past and future musical endeavors had and would receive.

Lennon played down his relationship with Ono to his wife. That is, until one day Cynthia came home from a trip to Greece to find the two together. Cynthia quickly gathered some belongings and ran out of her home into a taxi that had been waiting outside for her. She returned home a couple days later determined to make her marriage work. But it did not. Cynthia filed for divorce, which was finalized on November 8, 1968. She later married three more times.

Although they were no longer touring, the Beatles still were a band, albeit without a key member of their team. On August 27, 1967, the "fifth Beatle," as Brian Epstein often was called, was found dead at his home of a drug overdose. The Beatles were visiting with Transcendental

Although John and Yoko began their relationship as merely two artists who admired each other's work, they eventually grew closer, marrying in 1969 and spending the rest of Lennon's life together.

Meditation guru Maharishi Mahesh Yogi in Bangor, Wales, when they heard of his death. All four Beatles wondered what the future of the band might be.

Lennon's assessment proved to be spot on. Although holes had been forming in the Beatles' machine for some time, Epstein's death certainly hastened things. Plans had been in the works to form a business called Apple Corps to handle the Beatles' business affairs. The band members took on Apple's leadership role at first, until they discovered they could not handle the business end of things. So they hired their road manager, Neil Aspinall, to do so.

Much of the Beatles' best work was created the year Epstein died, including *Sgt. Pepper's Lonely Hearts Club Band*, the band's most experimental album to date. The occasionally psychedelic album was full of hits, including "Lucy in the Sky with Diamonds," "With a Little Help from My Friends," and "When I'm Sixty-Four." The album's cover featured wax models of the Beatles and the real Beatles posed among a collage of cardboard models of deceased famous people, including Edgar Allan Poe, Marilyn Monroe, and Albert Einstein. The album was followed by a movie of the same name, though none of the Beatles appeared in the film.

At the end of 1967, the Beatles released their *Magical Mystery Tour* album, which continued down the path of experimentation and drug-influenced music. For example, portions of "I Am the Walrus" were written when Lennon was high on LSD, and the lyrics of "Strawberry Fields Forever" talk about how "nothing is real." Other songs on the disc included the more-safe "Hello Goodbye," "All You Need Is Love," and "Penny Lane." The names Strawberry Field and Penny Lane were places drawn from the Beatles' childhood haunts in Liverpool. A made-for-TV film starring the Beatles called *Magical Mystery Tour* also was made.

The White Album

Recording sessions for the band's next album, simply titled *Beatles* but better known as *The White Album* because of its all-white cover, did not start off on the right foot. The band had a long-standing policy that wives and girlfriends were not allowed in the studio, but Ono came with Lennon to Abbey Road to record this album. She did not sit idly by, either; instead, she offered her critiques of the band members' performances and of the songs. Needless to say, the three other Beatles had big problems with Ono being there. They also had all been rather fond of Cynthia.

Though the band members' musical tastes had evolved quite a lot during the time they had been together, Lennon's experimental music did not sit well with the others. And McCartney's plainness drove Lennon up the wall. Harrison felt his songs were overlooked by the band as a whole, and Starr once became so upset that he walked out of the studio for two weeks, threatening to leave the band for good.

Despite all the internal tumult, *The White Album* was another masterpiece. It shot to the top of the charts when it was released in November 1968. It was the first full-length album the Beatles had released in nearly a year and a half. The band had released some material in that downtime, most notably "Hey Jude," a song McCartney wrote to Lennon's son, Julian, to help the five-year-old boy through the divorce of his parents. "Hey Jude" became the number one song in America and stayed there for several weeks.

By the summer of 1968, Lennon and Ono were completely open with their relationship and often appeared in public together. They moved into an apartment in London's Montagu Square, owned by Starr, where they began using drugs, including the often-deadly narcotic heroin. On October 18, 1968, police raided the

A MUSICAL DIVIDE

The songs on *The White Album* clearly showed the divide that existed between Lennon and McCartney. As it always was, most of the songwriting credits on the album were given to the team of Lennon/McCartney, but that was misleading this go-round. Each man basically wrote his own songs, using the other band members as a backing band to support them. McCartney highlights included "Back in the U.S.S.R.," "Ob-La-Di, Ob-La-Da," and the raucous "Helter Skelter." Lennon's songs included "Revolution 1," a slowed-down version of the up-tempo "Revolution" that had been released weeks earlier as the B-side to "Hey Jude," and "Julia," an acoustic song he had written about his mother that also included references to Yoko Ono. The double album format even gave the other Beatles room to showcase their tunes. Harrison's classic "While My Guitar Gently Weeps"—featuring Eric Clapton on lead guitar—among them.

apartment and found marijuana. The small amount of money Lennon eventually was fined after he pleaded guilty was negligible, but the damage to his once squeaky-clean reputation was not. Lennon later said he felt as if he was set up.

The Beatles still were not quite done. There was more music left in the band. In the spring of 1969, the band released *Yellow Submarine*, a mediocre album that was the soundtrack for a film of the same name. Later that year, they released *Abbey Road*, named after the studio it was made in. That album—which featured "Come Together," and two well-received Harrison songs, "Here Comes the Sun," and "Something"—was released in September.

Despite the controversy surrounding Lennon, the album still hit number one in both Britain and in the United States. The album cover, a photo of the band crossing the street to the studio, became one of the most-imitated photographs of all time. Today, there's even a Web cam set up nearby to record what is happening twenty-four hours a day at the popular tourist spot.

Once again, Yoko was by Lennon's side in the studio for this album, though she was a bit hobbled at first. Both Lennons had been injured in a car crash July 1, when John lost control of the car he was driving and it ended up in a ditch. John, Yoko, and Yoko's daughter, Kyoko, each had to have stitches to sew up cuts on their faces. Julian, who also had been in the car, was unharmed.

The Beginning of the End

Abbey Road was the last album the Beatles recorded together, but it was not the last Beatles studio album to be released. That distinction goes to *Let It Be*, which

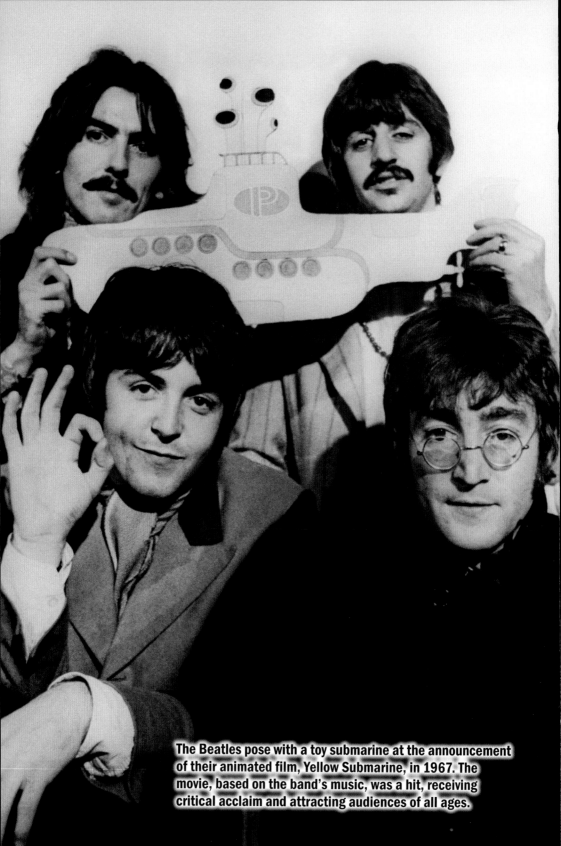

The Beatles pose with a toy submarine at the announcement of their animated film, Yellow Submarine, in 1967. The movie, based on the band's music, was a hit, receiving critical acclaim and attracting audiences of all ages.

the feuding band recorded in January 1969. When the recording was complete, the band was not happy with the final product, and shelved the tapes until a later date. In 1970, those tapes were given to producer Phil Spector, at the suggestion of Lennon, to turn into a finished album.

Spector had become well known for his "wall of sound" productions, whereby he would use several instruments playing the same part to create a layered sound. *Let It Be* was released to the public in May 1970, and rode its hit songs "Let It Be," "The Long and Winding Road," and "Get Back" to the top of the charts. Despite the album's success, McCartney in particular was angry that Spector had been hired to finish the album without his knowledge or consent. The album was supposed to have hearkened back to the band's roots, with simple music and not a lot of production. The released product was anything but that.

In 2003, a new version of the album without Spector's embellishments, called "Let It Be ... Naked," was released.

Film crews had been present to capture the rehearsing for and recording of *Let It Be*, and caught on tape the tension of the Beatles at the time. Ono again was omnipresent, and makes regular appearances in the film. The movie concludes with a short lunchtime concert performed January 30, 1969, on top of the Apple Corps building in London. Keyboardist Billy Preston, who had performed on *Let It Be*, sat in. With their long, shoulder-length hair, mustaches, and beards, the Beatles hardly resembled the squeaky clean lads they were when they burst on the scene some six years earlier. The concert ended when the police shut it down. It was the last time the Beatles performed together, and their official breakup was not far behind.

Out With McCartney, In With Ono

As indicated by her presence in the once-sacred recording studio, Ono was occupying most of Lennon's time at this point. In March, the pair flew to the British territory of Gibraltar, where they wed on March 20. Their honeymoon, as were most events the pair had become involved in, was unconventional. Lennon and Ono then traveled to Amsterdam, where they staged a week-long "bed-in for peace" in a hotel room. Reporters were invited to cover the event, which basically consisted of the Lennons lying in bed in their pajamas, talking about what they thought of war, peace, and more. The following month, Lennon legally changed his middle name, dropping the "Winston" and replacing it with "Ono." In May, in Montreal, Canada, the Lennons held a similar bed-in and then performed live at a peace concert in Toronto in September.

The Lennons' pro-peace message continued outside their bedroom, as well. In June, Lennon recorded, and the next month released, an antiwar song called "Give Peace a Chance," listing "The Plastic Ono Band" as the group's name. The song became a battle cry for the millions of US citizens who were protesting their country's involvement in the Vietnam War. In May, the Beatles released a single written and sung by Lennon called "The Ballad of John and Yoko." The song talked about the couple's marriage and their bed-in in Amsterdam. In October, Lennon released another single, "Cold Turkey," which talked about heroin addiction and withdrawals.

The peace-loving couple finished the year by installing eleven black-and-white billboards in major cities across the United States that read, "WAR IS OVER! IF YOU WANT IT: Happy Christmas from John & Yoko."

John Lennon and Yoko Ono held a "bed-in for peace" in 1969 to protest the Vietnam War. A few months later, the couple recorded the anti-war song "Give Peace a Chance."

If there was an "official" day that the Beatles breakup occurred, it was September 20, 1969. On that day, band members were gathered in London to sign a favorable new recording contract that had been negotiated by their new manager, Allen Klein.

When the four men began discussing what their next move would be, Lennon dropped a bombshell. McCartney recalled Lennon saying, "Well, I wasn't gonna tell you until after we'd signed the Capitol contract. Klein asked me not to tell you. But, seeing as you asked me, I'm leaving the group. . . . It's rather exciting. It's like I remember telling Cynthia I wanted a divorce."[3]

The band members kept Lennon's announcement under wraps for a while. But when word finally came out, it came from McCartney, which infuriated Lennon who believed McCartney was using the breakup to promote his own album. Included in the press kits for McCartney's first solo album, *McCartney*, released in April 1970, was a series of questions and answers with the artist. Reading McCartney's answers, there was no doubt the Beatles were through. The media went wild with the story, attributing the break up to McCartney leaving the Beatles. They had no idea that Lennon had quit months earlier.

Over the years, the breakup of the Beatles has been blamed on many things: poor business deals; McCartney's wife, Linda; George Harrison's quest for more musical input; drugs. But the most-frequently blamed reason was Yoko Ono, and many fans hated her for it.

6

Death of a Legend

The Beatles' breakup was final, and each individual member—George Harrison, Ringo Starr, and Paul McCartney—went about working on solo projects either for themselves or with others. Lennon eventually released more music, too, but he also spent his time pursuing other ventures. He had become fascinated by *The Primal Scream*, a book by California psychotherapist Arthur Janov, and he decided to fly to Los Angeles to work with Janov. He and Yoko spent a few months in California, participating in Janov's "Primal Scream" therapy class—where the patient would lie on the floor, think about bad events that had occurred in his or her life, and scream about them. The idea was to release all the pent-up pain and anger inside.

When he returned to England, Lennon began to refocus on music, and in December 1970, released his first solo album, *John Lennon/Plastic Ono Band*. The highly personal album includes songs about the loss of his mom—"Mother," and "My Mummy's Dead"—and others about abandonment, love, and religion. The album was praised by critics.

The nastiness of the Beatles' breakup came to a head in 1971, when McCartney sued to end the Beatles' partnership. A judge ruled in McCartney's favor a few

After leaving the Beatles, John performed regularly as a solo artist and with Yoko's group, The Plastic Ono Band. Here he's shown with Yoko onstage in New York in the 1970s.

years later. But the solo recordings kept coming. At the end of 1971, Lennon released his second, *Imagine*, which he had recorded at Tittenhurst, the expansive Georgian mansion outside London he and Yoko had moved into in 1969. As Lennon's previous release had been, *Imagine* was full of introspective and tender songs. Included among them was the title song, which continued Lennon's pro-peace message.

88

BONNIE AND CLYDE, JOHN AND YOKO

On April 23, 1971, John and Yoko tried to kidnap Yoko's daughter, Kyoko, from her father, Tony Cox, who had custody of the child. Detectives had tracked Cox to Spain, and the Lennons flew there and took Kyoko when she was at school. The police arrested the kidnappers and detained them for several hours. In the end, Kyoko was asked whom she would rather be with. It was exactly what had happened to Lennon when he was a child. Kyoko chose her father and her stepmother, and John and Yoko were released and flew back home.

Recording *Imagine* was one of the last noteworthy moves Lennon made at Tittenhurst, and even in England for that matter. By the time *Imagine* was released in early September, he and Yoko were in New York City. Escaping the stress the couple faced in England was one reason they were in New York; following Kyoko to the United States to continue trying to get custody of her was another. The Lennons soon moved to Greenwich Village in New York City, where they would hang out in their apartment with many of the leaders of the Youth

International Party (YIPPIE), a radical political group founded by activists such as Abbie Hoffman and Jerry Rubin. Drugs, including cocaine, heroin, and marijuana, were commonplace at the apartment.

The Lennons in the USA

Lennon's involvement with the left-wing group placed him under the watchful eye of the government, which wanted to deport him to England because they felt he was a threat to national security. The FBI even got involved, following Lennon around, tapping his phone, and filing reports on his activities. The government received thousands of letters of support for Lennon, and eventually backed off its calls for deportation.

Lennon had enough problems to deal with even without the government's harassment. His third solo album, 1972's angry *Some Time in New York City*, was a flop. Lennon's relationship with Yoko also was suffering. In an attempt to respark it, the couple moved from Greenwich Village to a luxurious apartment building near Central Park called the Dakota. The move did not help their relationship. The couple decided they needed a break from each other, and Yoko suggested John head to Los Angeles for a while. When he said he did not want to travel alone, she suggested he take their assistant, a twenty-two-year-old Chinese-American woman named May Pang. The trip did not turn out to be a short one.

Lennon and Pang spent much of the next fourteen months in Los Angeles, a period of time that Lennon would eventually call his "lost weekend." His fourth solo album, *Mind Games*, was released shortly after he arrived on the West Coast, and sold relatively well, especially

Following his marriage to Yoko and his departure from the Beatles, John moved to New York City, where he lived in a luxury apartment building on the edge of Central Park.

compared to his previous effort. His fifth solo album, 1974's *Walls and Bridges*, produced a number one single, a collaboration with pop musician Elton John called "Whatever Gets You Through the Night." The song even brought Lennon out of his unofficial retirement to again perform on stage, which he did with Elton John on Thanksgiving Day 1974, at Madison Square Garden in New York City.

Lennon and Pang returned to New York in February 1975, but they were not immediately welcomed back at the Dakota. Yoko still was not ready to live with her husband again, but eventually she caved in. Shortly after, she became pregnant, and on October 9, 1975, gave birth to Sean Taro Ono Lennon. The boy's first name was the Irish version of the name "John," and his middle name was the Japanese name commonly given to one's firstborn child. He was born on his father's thirty-fifth birthday to a forty-two-year-old mother who had stayed in bed during most of her pregnancy because of her advanced age and history of miscarriages.

Sean's birth domesticated Lennon, who shunned his old drinking and drugging buddies altogether, replacing them with days with his family inside their apartment. Even music took a backseat to the raising of Sean. After the release of *Rock 'n' Roll*, an album of Lennon singing 1950s- and 1960s-era songs, such as "Stand By Me," "Ain't That a Shame," and "Peggy Sue," Lennon mostly disappeared from the music scene, and did not release another album for five years. He even somewhat reconciled with McCartney, who would call and, eventually, stop by when he was in town.

In 1976, Lennon received his green card, allowing him to become a permanent United States resident. His next extended trip outside his apartment came a year later, when he, Sean, and Yoko traveled to Japan to spend time with Yoko's family. They spent four months there, basking in the freedom of not being recognized. When they returned to New York, Lennon continued doing many of the duties traditionally thought of as motherly. Sean, and age, had changed Lennon in many ways. In a sense he was now a recluse. To many, this made him even more

In 1975, John and Yoko welcomed a son, Sean Lennon. Following the birth of his second son, Lennon felt more settled, and was even inspired to reconcile with his former bandmate Paul McCartney.

fascinating than ever. Now, there was a mystery about him. Would he ever again perform in public? Would he release another album? Would the Beatles reunite?

One of the questions was answered in the fall of 1980, when Lennon released what was scheduled to be his big comeback record, *Double Fantasy*. The album featured eight of Yoko's songs and eight of Lennon's, mostly introspective pop songs. "(Just Like) Starting Over," and "Woman" were for Yoko; "Beautiful Boy (Darling Boy)" was for Sean; and "Watching the Wheels" was for his fans, a musical answer to the countless questions he received as to why he had taken so much time away from the spotlight. The album was a success. Lennon was inspired, and, on many days, made regular trips to the studio to record more music. December 8, 1980, was one such day.

John's Last Day

Lennon left the Dakota late in the day and headed out the front doors, stopping to sign a copy of *Double Fantasy* for a fan. Then he climbed into his limousine and rode to the studio. Some five hours later, Lennon returned home, climbed out of the limo, and headed back into the building. Before he entered, he heard a man call his name. Lennon turned to see who it was, and the man shot him five times in the back. Lennon wobbled into the Dakota's security office and moaned, "I'm shot, I'm shot."[1] When police arrived, Lennon was loaded into the back of a squad car and taken to the hospital. It was too late. He had lost too much blood, and he was pronounced dead on arrival. He was forty years old.

Back at the Dakota, Lennon's killer had sat on the sidewalk after the shooting, holding a copy of J. D.

John Lennon's murder was front-page news on December 9, 1980.

SPORTS FINAL

DAILY ◻ NEWS

★★★★ 25¢ NEW YORK, TUESDAY, DECEMBER 9, 1980 Rain. High 45 to 50. Details p. 68

JOHN LENNON SLAIN HERE

Ex-Beatle shot; nab suspect

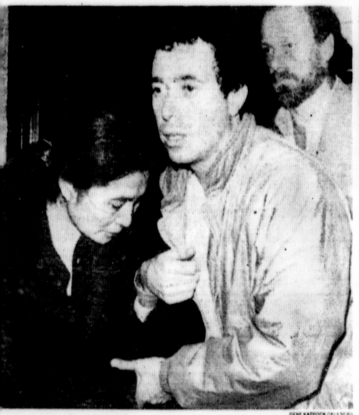

Killed outside his apartment

Yoko Ono, wife of former Beatle John Lennon, is helped from Roosevelt Hospital by record producer David Geffen after her husband was pronounced dead last night. Lennon was shot to death as he stepped from a car outside the Dakota apartment house on Central Park West where he lived. A suspect was taken into custody at the scene. Page 3

GENE KAPPOCK DAILY NEWS

Zingo! It's fun. 100G in prizes—Page 12

MCCARTNEY IN MOURNING

McCartney first learned of Lennon's death from a phone call. Reporters soon gathered at his home looking for comments, but even the next day, McCartney was too upset to speak much. He said, "I can't take it in at the moment. John was a great man, who'll be remembered for his unique contributions to art, music and world peace."[2] McCartney spent several days in the studio, focusing his mind on work to help keep it off the tragedy. He also worried for a long time that he might be the next Beatle to be killed.

Salinger's novel, *The Catcher in the Rye*. He did not resist as the police escorted him into a squad car. It was the same fan that, hours earlier, Lennon had signed a copy of his album for, Mark David Chapman, a twenty-five-year-old former security guard who had traveled from Hawaii to kill Lennon. Chapman later pleaded guilty to second-degree murder and was sentenced to twenty years to life in prison. He has come up for parole several times, and he has been denied each time.

Reaction to Lennon's death was immediate. TV stations interrupted their late-night broadcasts to announce what little information they had. Distraught and in shock, Yoko issued a brief statement saying that there would be no funeral.

Fans gathered in cities across the world to mourn the loss of the most-famous Beatle. In New York, thousands of people gathered outside the Dakota, singing "Give Peace a Chance," and other Lennon songs. Many camped out across the street in Central Park until the December 14 vigil, when more than one-hundred thousand people showed up. It was the largest mass mourning in the United States since 1963, when President John F. Kennedy was assassinated. Ironically, it had been the music of Lennon and the rest of the Beatles that helped the country's grieving process during that time.

Today, people still gather at Central Park on the anniversary of Lennon's death and on his birthday. In 1981, the City of New York voted to rename the two-and-one-half-acre portion of Central Park where fans gather as Strawberry Fields, after the Beatles song. A few years later, Yoko donated one million dollars to landscape and maintain the park. Today, Strawberry Fields features a large mosaic piece of art with the word "Imagine" in the middle of it.

CONCLUSION

usic helped many people heal after Lennon's death, including his three former bandmates. George Harrison wrote a song about Lennon, "All Those Years Ago," one year after Lennon's death, with Paul McCartney singing backing vocals. McCartney released his own tribute song, "Here Today," in 1982. Julian Lennon, who was seventeen at the time of his father's death, went on to become a musician, too, and wrote a song called "Too Late for Goodbyes" for his dad. Julian's half-brother, Sean, also began a career in music, both as a solo musician and as a member of others' bands.

The year after her husband's death, Yoko Ono began a romantic relationship with an antique-dealer-turned-artist named Sam Havadtoy, and she remained with him until 2001. She continued to release music and art projects, and she also worked to carry on the legacy of her late husband, no small task considering the legend he has become. That legacy includes handling Lennon's share of the Beatles' estate, which often led to her feuding with the other band members, especially McCartney, whom Lennon shared songwriting credits with. More recently, Yoko and McCartney have appeared together in public several times.

McCartney continued on with his music, as well, and went on to become the most successful songwriter in history, having written or co-written 188 records that made it on the charts.

Harrison released a total of eleven solo albums after the Beatles broke up, and he had a few number one singles. In the late 1980s, he formed a rock-and-roll supergroup, called the Traveling Wilburys, with Bob Dylan, Jeff Lynne, Roy Orbison, and Tom Petty. In 2002, another all-star band—including McCartney and Starr—formed to honor Harrison, who had died of brain cancer on November 29, 2001, at the age of fifty-eight.

Like the other Beatles, Starr continued releasing music after Lennon's death, even touring with several different lineups under the name Ringo Starr & His All-Starr Band. In the mid-1980s, he acted as both narrator and conductor of the popular TV show, *Thomas the Tank Engine and Friends*, and he also has been involved in numerous film projects—as an actor, producer, director, and more.

Julian Lennon (right) is joined by (from left) Sean Lennon, Yoko Ono, and mother Cynthia Powell at the opening of his "Timeless" photo exhibition in 2010 in New York City.

In the years immediately following Lennon's death, fans continued to clamor for a reunion of the remaining Beatles. It never happened. However, the three remaining Beatles did reunite in the studio once, in 1994. That happened after Yoko gave the band members some tapes of songs Lennon had recorded years earlier. The Beatles took the tapes, recorded their own parts to them, and completed two songs: "Free as a Bird," and "Real Love." The songs were released in the mid-1990s on separate *Anthology* compilation albums. That same year, Lennon

On what would have been John Lennon's seventy-fifth birthday, a tribute concert was held. Musicians Tom Morello, Kris Kristofferson, and Mickey Raphael (from left) were among the performers.

was inducted into the Rock and Roll Hall of Fame as a solo artist. The Beatles had received the same honor six years earlier.

The Beatles now have sold more than 180 million records in the United States alone. That is 50 million more than Elvis Presley, the man whose music helped inspire each of the Beatles to begin playing music in the first place, and the person Lennon said he always aspired to be bigger than. He succeeded in that quest. Worldwide, the Beatles have sold almost two billion records. Both those sales numbers are world records, and they are not the only ones the band holds. In 2000, the Beatles set another record when they sold 13.5 million copies of their album *1*, which featured nearly every song the band released that had topped either the US or British sales charts.

In death, John Lennon has become an icon. How different might music, and perhaps the world, be if a crazed fan had not prematurely ended Lennon's life? All one can do is imagine.

CHRONOLOGY

1940 John Winston Lennon is born October 9 in Liverpool, England, to Alfred "Alf" and Julia Lennon. Ringo Starr is born.

1942 James Paul McCartney is born.

1943 George Harold Harrison is born.

1945 John's parents separate; John goes to live with his aunt and uncle, George and Mimi Smith, at Mendips.

1952 John enters Quarry Bank High School.

1955 John's uncle, George Smith, dies.

1956 John's mother buys John his first guitar and he forms first band, eventually to be known as The Quarrymen.

1957 John meets Paul McCartney and asks him to join group; begins attending Liverpool College of Art.

1958 John meets George Harrison and asks him to join group; records music for first time; mother, Julia, struck and killed by automobile.

1960 Stuart Sutcliffe and Pete Best join The Quarrymen; band changes its name to the Beatles; Beatles begin residency in Hamburg, Germany.

1961 Stuart Sutcliffe quits the band, necessitating Paul McCartney's switch from guitar to bass; Beatles meet future manager Brian Epstein.

1962 Stuart Sutcliffe dies; Ringo Starr replaces Pete Best on drums; Lennon weds longtime girlfriend Cynthia Powell.

1963 First Beatles album, *Please Please Me,* is released; son John Charles Julian Lennon is born April 8.

1964 Beatles perform on *The Ed Sullivan Show* and begin first tour of United States; Lennon publishes first book, *In His Own Write.*

1965 Lennon publishes second book, *A Spaniard in the Works.*

1966 Lennon is criticized for saying the Beatles are "more popular than Jesus"; plays role in film, *How I Won the War*; meets artist Yoko Ono.

1967 Beatles manager Brian Epstein dies of drug overdose.

1968 Divorce from Cynthia is finalized; Lennon is arrested, along with Yoko Ono, for drug possession; releases experimental album with Ono called *Two Virgins.*

1969 Lennon marries Yoko Ono; stages two "bed-ins for peace" with Yoko Ono; Beatles officially break up; Lennon records "Give Peace a Chance" with Ono.

1970 Lennon releases first solo album, *John Lennon/Plastic Ono Band.*

1971 Lennon releases second solo album, *Imagine*; moves to New York City.

1972 Lennon releases third solo album, *Some Time in New York City*; FBI begins monitoring Lennon's activities.

1973 Lennon separates from Yoko Ono and moves to Los Angeles with assistant May Pang.

1975 Lennon moves back to New York apartment with Yoko Ono; son Sean Taro Ono Lennon is born October 9.

1976 Lennon receives his green card, allowing him to become a permanent resident of the United States.

1980 Releases *Double Fantasy* album; shot and killed outside his apartment by Mark David Chapman on December 8.

1988 Beatles inducted into Rock and Roll Hall of Fame.

1994 Lennon inducted into Rock and Roll Hall of Fame as a solo artist.

CHAPTER NOTES

Introduction

1. Phillip Norman, *John Lennon: The Life* (New York: HarperCollins, 2008), p. 343.
2. "The Beatles: The First U.S. Visit," August 14, 2007, <http://www.youtube.com/ watch?v=jYciRQDkYD4> (July 6, 2009).
3. Jann S. Wenner, *Lennon Remembers* (London: Verso, 2000), p. 20.

Chapter 1: Genius and Pain

1. Bob Spitz, *The Beatles: The Biography* (New York: Little, Brown and Company, 2005), p. 28.
2. Ibid.
3. Hunter Davies, *The Beatles* (London: Cassell Illustrated, 1996), p. 12.
4. Julia Baird with Geoffrey Giuliano, *John Lennon, My Brother* (New York: Henry Holt and Co., 1988), p. 13.
5. Peter Shotton and Nicholas Schaffner, *John Lennon in My Life* (New York: Stein and Day, 1983), p. 31.
6. Ibid, p. 49.
7. Shotton and Schaffner, p. 67.
8. Beatles, *The Beatles Anthology* (San Francisco: Chronicle, 2000), p. 12.

Chapter 2: Becoming the Beatles

1. Julia Baird with Geoffrey Giuliano, *John Lennon, My Brother* (New York: Henry Holt and Co., 1988), p. 44.
2. Ibid.
3. Pete Best and Patrick Doncaster, *Beatle! The Pete Best Story* (London: Plexus, 2001), p. 13.

Chapter 3: Made in Germany

1. Hunter Davies, *The Beatles* (London: Cassell Illustrated, 1996), p. 43.

2. Davies, pp. 92–93.

3. Pete Best and Patrick Doncaster, *Beatle! The Pete Best Story* (London: Plexus, 2001), p. 83.

4. Ray Coleman, *Lennon: The Definitive Biography* (London: Pan Books, 1992), p. 251.

5. Phillip Norman, *John Lennon: The Life* (New York: HarperCollins, 2008), p. 263.

Chapter 4: Beatlemania Spreads

1. Bob Spitz, *The Beatles: The Biography* (New York: Little, Brown and Company, 2005), p. 497.

2. Ibid.

3. Casey McNerthney, "Beatles stay at Edgewater helped mark its place in history," *The Seattle Post-Intelligencer*, August 20, 2009, <http://www. seattlepi.com/local/409468_beatles21.html> (August 21, 2009).

Chapter 5: "More Popular Than Jesus"

1. Bob Spitz, *The Beatles: The Biography* (New York: Little, Brown and Company, 2005), p. 615.

2. Phillip Norman, *John Lennon: The Life* (New York: HarperCollins, 2008), p. 466.

3. Barry Miles, *Paul McCartney: Many Years From Now* (New York: Henry Holt and Co., 1997), p. 561.

Chapter 6: Death of a Legend

1. Ray Coleman, *Lennon: The Definitive Biography* (London: Pan Books, 1995), p. 701.

2. Miles, p. 593.

FURTHER READING

Books

Burger, Jeff. *Lennon on Lennon: Conversations With John Lennon*. New York, NY: Omnibus, 2017.

Sheffield, Rob. *Dreaming the Beatles: The Love Story of One Band and the Whole World*. New York, NY: HarperCollins, 2017.

Turner, Steve. *Beatles '66: The Revolutionary Year*. New York, NY: HarperCollins, 2017.

Websites

John Lennon

www.johnlennon.com

Features John Lennon merchandise and music, as well as links to his artworks and writings.

Rolling Stone Magazine

www.rollingstone.com

A music news website that features stories about John Lennon and the Beatles, both from years past as well as current stories and photos of the surviving band members.

Films

Leaf, David and John Scheinfeld. *The U.S. vs. John Lennon*. Lions Gate, 2007.

Solt, Andrew. *Imagine: John Lennon*. WarnerBrothers, 2005.

GLOSSARY

avant-garde Experimental.

controversy An incident or event that causes people to question the rightness or motives of a person, group, or experience. Yoko Ono's influence on John Lennon caused controversy for the Beatles when they broke up.

corporal punishment Physical punishment exacted on someone accused of a crime.

The Ed Sullivan Show A popular evening talk and variety show that ran weekly from 1948 until 1971. The show is famous for introducing American audiences to the Beatles, as well as for Elvis Presley's defining hip-shaking performance.

experimental music Music that doesn't fit a genre and often is composed of strange or unconventional sounds and rhythms. Yoko Ono is particularly known for the experimental sound of her music.

extramarital Something occurring outside the marriage, such as an affair.

green card A document given to an individual allowing him or her to become a permanent resident of the United States.

hemorrhage A discharge of a large amount of blood from the blood vessels.

introspection The act of examining one's own feelings and thoughts.

mastectomy Surgical removal of all or part of a breast, often performed as a treatment for cancer.

single A song that is released on its own. Sometimes this is a song from an album that is released as a special single; other times, artists may release a single as a one-off song when they don't have an album to include the song on.

skiffle A style of music featuring rudimentary instruments such as washboards and jugs popular in Britain during the 1950s.

stucco A type of plaster or cement finish used on the inside or outside wall of a home.

subsidiary A company that is subordinate to another.

Teddy boy The name given to rebellious British youth of the 1950s who often wore long jackets, skinny ties, and short-legged pants.

tour A series of concerts performed by a musician while traveling. Each concert is a "stop" on the tour, and the entire tour can last for weeks, months, or years, spanning cities, states, countries, or the world.

INDEX